R

AND PRAYERS

FOR VISITS WITH OUR
EUCHARISTIC LORD

by John J. Cardinal Carberry

Pauline
BOOKS & MEDIA
Boston

ISBN 0-8198-6436-6

Cover design by Rosana Usselmann

Cover photo by Mary Emmanuel Alves, FSP

"P" and PAULINE are registered trademarks of the Daughters of St. Paul.

Published by Pauline Books & Media, 50 Saint Pauls Avenue, Boston, MA 02130-3491

Printed in the U.S.A

www.pauline.org

Pauline Books & Media is the publishing house of the Daughters of St. Paul, an international congregation of women religious serving the Church with the communications media.

19 20 21 22 23   19 18 17 16 15 14

CONTENTS

FOREWORD

In his encyclical letter, *Mysterium Fidei* (September 3, 1965), Pope Paul VI describes the graces and blessings that await those who manage to find time to visit our divine Lord in the most Blessed Sacrament:

"Christ is truly Emmanuel, that is, 'God with us.' Day and night, he is in our midst; he dwells with us full of grace and truth. He restores morality, nourishes virtue, consoles the afflicted, and strengthens the weak. He proposes his own example to those who come to him that they may learn to be like himself, meek and humble of heart, and to seek not their own interest, but the things of God. Anyone, therefore, who approaches this august sacrament with special devotion and endeavors to return generous love for Christ's infinite love, experiences and fully understands, not without great spiritual joy and profit, how precious is the life hidden with Christ in God and how great is the value of converse with Christ, for there is nothing more consoling on earth, nothing more efficacious for advancing along the road to holiness."

Many willing souls have a desire to dwell in prayer with our Eucharistic Lord, but often they are at a loss as to how to spend their time. This booklet attempts to supply thoughts as well as prayers that may prove helpful during a visit with Jesus in the most Blessed Sacrament. For over thirty years, I have gathered notes in preparation for the publication of these reflections before the tabernacle, but these remained in manuscript and were never completed. In the hope, however, that priests, religious, and laity may be helped by them, they are now submitted in this present form. The years of delay had a purpose, for now more than ever, there is a need to encourage and help souls to spend some time with our Eucharistic Lord in prayer and reflection.

It is with a spirit of admiration and gratitude that I prayerfully dedicate these pages to the Legion of One Thousand Men,* which flourishes in the Archdiocese of St. Louis. Started by Joseph Cardinal Ritter, of blessed memory and my beloved predecessor, it has continued in strength over the years.

The men of the Legion make a simple pledge, namely to visit once a week one of the three monasteries where the most Blessed Sacrament is exposed daily. There is no

---

* This group has since been expanded to include women and is now called the Legion of One Thousand Adorers. *Ed.*

specified time of day for the visit, nor length of time to remain. Each man signs a card with his name and parish after the visit, so that an estimate can be made weekly of how many visits have been made. Since there are three monasteries with a Legion of a Thousand Men attached to each, the actual number of weekly visits is more than four thousand and sometimes reaches five.

It has been an inspiration to me, as well as for many others, to see the constant stream of men coming and going to commune with our dear Lord in the most Blessed Sacrament. Only God knows the graces that come to them personally, to their families, and to the Archdiocese from their dedication and devotion to our Eucharistic Lord.

I humbly ask Our Lady of the Most Blessed Sacrament to bless this effort of mine and through it to bring many to understand the strength, peace, courage, light and understanding, grace and renewal, which can be experienced through silent prayer in the presence of Jesus, who is Emmanuel, that is, "God is with us."

PREFACE

Several years have passed since this booklet was first printed in July 1971. Over these years experience has pointed out several ways in which it might be restudied to widen its appeal. Finally, after prayer and consultation, I believe that that time has come to gather the various ideas and to present them in the present form with the hope that they will be beneficial for bringing souls more closely and more personally to our dear Lord in the most Blessed Sacrament.

It will be noted, at once, that the format has been changed to that of a pocket-size booklet so that it can be carried easily and be more available whenever one visits our dear Lord or even wishes to use the prayers for other occasions, such as at home, or as a means of thanksgiving after Holy Communion.

A new section on visits to our Blessed Lady has been introduced. It is hoped that Mary, Our Lady of the Most Blessed Sacrament, will be a source of inspiration, comfort, and consolation to those who use this booklet. The prayer "All through the heart of Mary in honor of the most Blessed Sacrament" summarizes the intimate union there is between the love of Christ, our Eucharistic King, and his loving Mother Mary.

At the conclusion of each of the main divisions of the booklet, namely adoration, sorrow, thanksgiving, and petition, several verses from Sacred Scripture have been added as a source of meditation. The context from which the verse has been taken is given so that one might read the entire passage from the Word of God, if so desired. Often a simple passage of Sacred Scripture is sufficient for prayerful reflection, which over time reveals its depth and beauty more and more. The prayers in the booklet have been rearranged and additional prayers have been added.

In a spirit of humility I place this revised edition in the hands of our loving Mother Mary and ask her to awaken and deepen in the hearts of all a desire to know, love, and serve her divine son, Jesus. He is for everyone the beginning and end of all things; he is for us the God-Man; he is for us the Way, Truth, and Life.

✠ JOHN JOSEPH CARDINAL CARBERRY
Retired Archbishop of St. Louis
December 8, 1977
Feast of the Immaculate Conception of Our Lady

WAYS TO USE THIS BOOKLET

This booklet has three main divisions. The first part contains thoughts that may assist one in communing with our dear Lord in the most Blessed Sacrament, either exposed for adoration or in the tabernacle. These thoughts are chiefly centered on the themes of prayer—namely, adoration, thanksgiving, sorrow, and petition. In addition, there are reflections for the beginning and the conclusion of a visit.

It is important to note that the ideas set forth in this first part are intended to offer material that one may develop for personal prayer and reflection. *They are to be read slowly and followed with occasional pauses for meditation and application. Actually, they are intended to help one pray, rather than to be prayers in themselves.*

The second part is devoted to prayers to our dear Blessed Lady, Mother of the Savior who lives in the Eucharist. We receive God's graces through Mary's maternal intercession. The recitation of the rosary is a great help for a Eucharistic visit. As one recites the Hail Mary, one can meditate on the mysteries of the life of Jesus, present in the Blessed Sacrament.

Another help to prayer and reflection will be found in the suggested readings from the New Testament, the inspired Word of God. These readings are found at the end of each section in Part I and Part II. While a few verses are given in this booklet, the whole passage cited can be read from a Bible. The Jesus about whom we read, whose words are echoing in our mind, is the same Jesus present before us. We are in his divine presence—this is the mystery of our faith. The words and actions of our Blessed Lord can stir up in us prayers of adoration, thanksgiving, sorrow, and petition as we read and meditate upon Sacred Scripture in his adorable presence.

The third part of the booklet contains additional prayers for devotional use, along with a wider selection of suggested readings from Sacred Scripture.

This booklet is merely an instrument, used as one may wish, beginning at the end, or in the center, or at the beginning. In the visit to the Blessed Sacrament it is not necessary to kneel all the time; rather one is free to stand or to sit. A sense of relaxation is of the greatest importance—a sense of being at home with a changeless Friend, our Lord and our God. No particular amount of time is required for the visit. That depends on circumstances. With frequent use of the booklet it may become easy to make the visit a little longer, for it may succeed in opening new vistas of prayer and reflection. When we leave all in the loving hands of the dear Lord, he gives us the grace of understanding and communing with him.

One final word: it does not really matter how we may feel during our visit with our Savior. Feelings of joy, peace, comfort, strength, and consolation are helpful and they often come as a gift to us. What matters is that we, by our visit to him, express in word and deed our faith, our hope, and our love. We never leave him without his special blessing upon us and a particular grace of favor.

Part I

REFLECTIONS FOR VISITS

Opening Thoughts

Coming from home, business, or other concerns, my first thoughts for my visit to the most Blessed Sacrament should help me to cross the "bridge," as it were, between the outside world and this sacred sanctuary where my Lord and God is awaiting me and in whose presence I now kneel. Therefore, to help me cross this bridge and place myself in his divine presence, the following may be useful.

Why am I here?

Jesus gives me the answer: "Come to me, all you that are weary and are carrying heavy burdens, and I will give you rest" (Mt 11:28).

I have come, my Lord and King, to be with you, to call to mind the great mystery of faith: your presence, body and blood, soul and divinity, in the consecrated bread of life. Let me recall more carefully how I can realize my visit in response to your invitation—"Come to me. . . ."

I have come *to adore you, Jesus,* by acts of faith, hope, and love; to express *sorrow for my sins;* to make *reparation for the sins of the world;* to thank you *for your blessings,* so many of which I take for granted; and to present to you my needs, spiritual and temporal, as well as the needs of all who are near and dear to me and who have requested my prayers.

I have come to you with loving confidence recalling your words: "Ask, and it will be given you; search, and you will find; knock, and the door will be opened for you. For everyone who asks receives, and everyone who searches finds, and for everyone who knocks, the door will be opened" (Mt 7:7–9).

Help me, most loving Mother Mary, to spend this time of quiet prayer profitably—in the presence of Jesus.

Intentions for My Visit

During this time of prayer I want to remember especially *N. N.* To make sure that my visit is profitable, I shall pray to the Holy Spirit of light and truth, of consolation and comfort:

Come, Holy Spirit, fill the hearts of your faithful and enkindle in them the fire of your divine love. Send forth your Spirit and they shall be created, and you shall renew the face of the earth.

Let Us Pray

O God, who has taught the hearts of the faithful by the light of the Holy Spirit, grant that by that same Holy Spirit we may become truly wise and ever rejoice in his consolation, through Christ our Lord. Amen.

I also ask our Blessed Mother, Our Lady of the Most Blessed Sacrament, the Temple of the Holy Spirit, to be with me as I visit her divine Son. I ask her to be my companion and to help supply for my deficiencies:

O my dear Mother, behold me, your child, blessed with the grace of spending this time in prayer before your most loving and divine Son.

I turn to you with earnest prayer for help and assistance. In your life upon earth and now in heaven, your joy has ever been to spend time in his blessed company. Assist me to spend this time well in loving and prayerful devotion, to avoid distractions and worry, and to leave with my soul inflamed by the love of Jesus.

Accept my feeble thoughts and weak words of adoration, love, and sorrow. Transform them into your sentiments so that they will be acceptable in the sight of your divine Son. O Mary, my Mother, my Queen of the Most Blessed Sacrament, help me.

I am all yours, O most loving Jesus, and all I have I offer to you through Mary, your Holy Mother. Reveal your divine Son to me, O Mary. Make me love him as you did and inspire me to live for him.

∽ *Pause • Reflect • Pray* ∽

A. Prayer of Adoration

In the prayer of adoration, I seek to realize the greatness of God, my Creator and my last end. When I enter into the depths of my soul and ponder who God is and who I am, almost instinctively I kneel and express sentiments of my faith in God, my hope and trust in God, and above all, my love for God.

When Christ appeared to his apostles on the Sea of Galilee after his resurrection, Saint John recognized him and said: "It is the Lord" (Jn 21:7). I ask, dear Jesus, for the grace to appreciate your presence, saying: "It is the Lord," and in the words of Saint Peter add: "You are the Messiah, the Son of the living God" (Mt 16:16).

In Whose Presence Am I?

I am not in an audience with our Holy Father, nor am I in the presence of a saint from heaven, nor with some distinguished personality. Before me, dear Jesus, you are present under the frail appearance of the host. With the eyes of faith I believe that you are present as my God, my Lord, my Redeemer, the Creator of heaven and earth, my *all*. I believe, dear Jesus, that you are truly present, body and blood, soul and divinity, in the most Blessed Sacrament.

My Response

With your grace I wish to pour forth from the depths of my heart sentiments of faith, hope, and love for you, Jesus, my Eucharistic Lord. At times I may not be able to find words to express the sentiments of my heart. At times I will be distracted and perhaps feel weariness and dryness. If that happens, I will kneel in silence before you, aware that you know the innermost thoughts of my mind and the earnest desires of my heart. The thoughts and prayers of others may greatly help me in finding the words that will express my great love for you.

∽ *Pause • Reflect • Pray* ∾

Act of Adoration

Jesus, my God, I adore you here present in the Blessed Sacrament of the altar, where you wait day and night to be our comfort while we await your unveiled presence in heaven. Jesus, my God, I adore you in all places where the Blessed Sacrament is reserved, and where sins are committed against this Sacrament of love. Jesus, my God, I adore you for all time, past, present, and future, for every soul that ever was, is, or shall be created. Jesus, my God, who for us endured hunger and cold, labor and fatigue, I adore you. Jesus, my God, who for my sake deigned to subject yourself to the humiliation of temptation, to the betrayal and defection of friends, to the scorn of your enemies, I adore you. Jesus, my God, who for us endured the buffeting of your passion, the scourging, the crowning with thorns, the heavy weight of the cross, I adore you. Jesus, my God, who, for my salvation and that of the whole human race, was cruelly nailed to the cross and hung there for three long hours in bitter agony, I adore you. Jesus, my God, who for love of us instituted this Blessed Sacrament and offered your life for the sins of the whole world, I adore you. Jesus, my God, who in Holy Communion became the food of my soul, I adore you.

Jesus, for you I live. Jesus, for you I die. Jesus, I am yours in life and death. Amen.

Act of Faith

O Christ Jesus! True God and man, of one substance, majesty, and power with the Father, with firm faith I believe and confess that you are truly and really present in this Sacrament. For you, who are Truth itself, have said, "This is my body."

Act of Hope

O God, my hope! My heart rejoices when I receive you in the Blessed Sacrament, because I clearly trust that there is nothing that you have not given us and will not give us. In you, O Lord, I trust; let me not be confounded in my hope.

Act of Love

I love you, O Christ Jesus, because in your exceeding love for me, you have come in the flesh and have loved me even to death, and in the Blessed Sacrament have given me yourself for a pledge of this love. I love you more than myself and more than all things; at least, I most earnestly desire so to love you and always to adhere to you alone. O, by the power of this sacrament may there be cemented between you and me a union of love so great that nothing may be able to separate me from the love of Christ my Savior.

A Spiritual Communion

My Jesus, I believe that you are present in the most Holy Sacrament. I love you above all things and I desire to receive you into my soul. Since I cannot at this moment receive you sacramentally, come at least spiritually into my heart. I embrace you as if you were already there and I unite myself wholly to you; never permit me to be separated from you.

Prayer of Saint Thomas More

Give me the grace to long for your holy sacraments, and especially to rejoice in the presence of your Body, sweet Savior Christ, in the Holy Sacrament of the altar. Amen.

Suggested Readings from the New Testament

" . . . We observed his star at its rising, and have come to pay him homage." [A]nd there, ahead of them, went the star that they had seen at its rising, until it stopped over the place where the child was. (Mt 2:1–12)

[Jesus] was transfigured before them, and his face shone like the sun, and his clothes became dazzling white. . . . Suddenly a bright cloud overshadowed them, and from the cloud a voice said, "This is my Son, the Beloved; with him I am well pleased; listen to him!" (Mt 17:1–8)

. . . And suddenly there was with the angel a multitude of the heavenly host, praising God and saying, "Glory to God in the highest heaven, and on earth peace among those whom he favors!" (Lk 2:8–20)

. . . Jesus came and stood among them and said, "Peace be with you." Then he said to Thomas, "Put your finger here and see my hands. Reach out your hand and

put it in my side. Do not doubt but believe." Thomas
answered him, "My Lord and my God!" (Jn 20:24–29)

B. Prayer of Sorrow

*"A broken and contrite heart, O God, you will not despise" (Ps
51:17). These words express the meaning of prayer and sorrow. By
means of it, I look at myself: I see my failings, my sins, my weaknesses.
"God opposes the proud, but gives grace to the humble" (1 Pt 5:5). In
addition, I glance at the world around me—with its sins and forgetfulness of God. In the prayer of sorrow, I try to express my sorrow for my
personal sins and to offer reparation for the sins of the world.*

Jesus, My Redeemer

Beloved Jesus, may I ever be conscious of the fact that
I am in your adorable presence—I am in the presence of
you who by your life, death, and resurrection, paid the
price of my sins and the sins of the world. May I always
be open to receive this gift by a life of continual faith and
love.

Sorrow for My Sins

Through sorrow for sin, expressed in the sacrament
of Penance, you forgive my sins, my Eucharistic Lord.
However, I want to always be conscious of that sorrow
and to renew it as often as possible without torment-

ing my soul. How often Saint Peter and Saint Mary Magdalene must have thought of their sins and expressed their grief to you. As I glance at my life since my last confession and examine my conscience, how many failings I can now see, which I have forgotten or overlooked. How often I fall into the same sins! And yet, there is no end to your merciful forgiveness. With all my heart and soul I express to you, my beloved Savior, sorrow for my sins and my desire to always seek purity of heart:

Lord Jesus Christ, you are the Lamb of God;
  you take away the sins of the world.
Through the grace of the Holy Spirit restore me
    to friendship with your Father,
cleanse me from every stain of sin through the blood
    you shed for me,
and raise me to new life for the glory of your name.

Reparation for the Sins of the World

Everywhere I see evidence of sin: crime, persecutions, forgetfulness and denial of God, rebellion against the law of God. These present such a sad sight. I shall renew my personal love for you, Jesus, and rededicate my life to you. I will endeavor to accept the crosses that come into my life— sickness, ingratitude, neglect, trials of all kinds, misunderstandings, the uncertainties of life and temptations against faith. I will endeavor to bear all my sufferings patiently, with Christian joy, and to unite my suffering with yours. My Eucharistic Jesus, I earnestly pray the following Act of Reparation that expresses the sentiments of my soul:

Eternal Father, I offer you the Holy Face of Jesus covered with blood, sweat, dust, and spittle in reparation for the sins of blasphemy, of disrespect for the Holy Name of Jesus, and for failing to honor Sunday as the Lord's day. May the most holy, most sacred, most adorable, most mysterious and unutterable name of God always be praised, blessed, loved, adored, and glorified in heaven, on earth and under the earth, by all the creatures of God. May the Sacred Heart of our Lord Jesus Christ in the Most Holy Sacrament of the altar always be praised, adored, and loved. Amen.

Suggested Readings from Sacred Scripture

> . . . [Peter] began to curse, and he swore an oath, "I do not know the man!" At that moment the cock crowed. Then Peter remembered what Jesus had said: "Before the cock crows, you will deny me three times." And he went out and wept bitterly. (Mt 26:69–75)

> The Pharisees and their scribes were complaining to his disciples, saying, "Why do you eat and drink with tax collectors and sinners?" Jesus answered, "Those who

are well have no need of a physician, but those who are sick; I have come to call not the righteous but sinners to repentance." (Lk 5:27–32)

[Jesus said] . . ."Do you think that because these Galileans suffered in this way they were worse sinners than all other Galileans? No, I tell you; but unless you repent, you will all perish as they did." (Lk 13:1–5)

"Just so, I tell you, there will be more joy in heaven over one sinner who repents than over ninety-nine righteous persons who need no repentance." (Lk 15:7)

"Submit yourselves therefore to God. Resist the devil, and he will flee from you. . . . Lament and mourn and weep. . . . Humble yourselves before the Lord, and he will exalt you." (Jas 4:6–10)

∞ *Pause • Reflect • Pray* ∞

C. Prayer of Thanksgiving

One of the main purposes of prayer is to thank you, God, for your goodness, your blessings and your gifts to me. In your divine presence I will try to recall how much I owe you, and I will ask our Lady to help me express my gratitude to you. As I kneel in quiet prayer let me review with appreciation some of my many reasons for gratitude.

∞ *Pause • Reflect • Pray* ∞

God's Natural Blessings

I thank you:

For the gift of life and every moment I live.

For my health, even though at times I may have been ill or suffered from chronic conditions and pain. So often these and other crosses are blessings in disguise.

For the world about me, the glories of nature, the moon, the stars, the flowers of the fields, the fruits of the earth, the glorious sunshine, the seasons of the year.

For my parents, my relatives, my treasured and trusted friends.

God's Supernatural Blessings

I thank you:

For the gift of faith.

For the gift of yourself in the Incarnation in which you became man, lived for me, and taught me by your words and example.

For the gift of redemption, which you accomplished by your sufferings, death, and resurrection—all this for my salvation.

For the graces of the sacraments, especially my Baptism and Confirmation.

For the consolation of the sacrament of Reconciliation.

For the joy of the Holy Eucharist.

For the graces of Holy Orders (*if I am a priest*).

For the graces of Matrimony (*if I am married*).

For the graces of the single state (*if I am not married*).

For the comfort of a last Anointing (*when I need it*).

∞ *Pause • Reflect • Pray* ∞

Act of Thanksgiving

I recall the incident of the ten lepers: When only one returned to thank you, Lord, you said: "Were not ten made clean? But the other nine, where are they?" (Lk 17:17). Am I not often among those who receive gifts from God, rejoice in them, but forget my benefactor? To help me acquire the habit of saying "Thanks be to God for his graces and blessings," I will offer the following prayer:

O my God, I thank you for all the favors you have bestowed upon me. I give you thanks from the bottom of my heart for having created me, and for all the joys of life and its sorrows, too, for the home you gave me, for the loved ones with which you have surrounded me, for the friends I have made through life.

My Lord, I thank you for guarding me always and keeping me safe; I thank you for forgiving my sins so often in the sacrament of Penance; for offering yourself in Holy Mass, with all your infinite merits, to the Father for me and for all of us; for coming to me in Holy Communion, in spite of the coldness of my welcome; for your patient waiting in the adorable sacrament of the altar.

My Jesus, I thank you for having lived, suffered, and died for me. I thank you for your love. I thank you, Lord, for preparing a place for me in heaven where I hope to be happy with you and to thank you for all eternity. Amen.

Suggested Readings from Sacred Scripture

. . . The crowd was amazed when they saw the mute speaking, the maimed whole, the lame walking, and the blind seeing. And they praised the God of Israel. (Mt 15:29–31)

[Jesus] took a loaf of bread, and after blessing it he broke it, gave it to them, and said, "Take; this is my body." Then he took a cup, and after giving thanks he gave it to them, and all of them drank from it. He said to them, "This is my blood of the covenant, which is poured out for many." (Mk 14:22–25)

Simeon took [the child Jesus] in his arms and praised God, saying, "Master, now you are dismissing your servant in peace, according to your word." (Lk 2:25–32)

. . . One of them, when he saw that he was healed, turned back, praising God with a loud voice. He prostrated himself at Jesus' feet and thanked him. (Lk 17:11–19)

D. Prayer of Petition

This form of prayer is readily understood. In fact, many often think of it as the only way to pray! Yet it is only a part of prayer, coming after the other forms of adoration, thanksgiving, and sorrow. My prayer of petition must be based on a firm faith and guided by a spirit of openness to God's will. Christ said: "Ask, and it will be given you" (Mt 7:7). There are no limits. God is waiting. This is my opportunity to present my needs to God—whether spiritual or temporal, for body or for soul. So many things are needed for myself, for others, and for the world.

General Intentions

Peace:

In my own heart, in my home, in the Church, and in the world.

The reign of Christ in the hearts of all people:

That people everywhere will come to know, love, and serve you, my dear Jesus, and realize that you are our Lord and God.

Conversion of sinners:

That all those touched by God's grace will respond, repent, and come to know the joy of a heart at peace with God.

Christian unity:

"That all may be one," in fulfillment of your prayer, dear Jesus, at the Last Supper.

Social justice:

That all of us in your Spirit will be brothers and sisters so that racial discrimination will disappear. That all of us will help the poor, the suffering, the downtrodden.

That law and order will be observed by everyone. That crime and immorality in the world will decrease and disappear.

For the protection of all human life, from conception to natural death.

The Church Universal:

That God may bless, guide, and strengthen the Pope in his labors.

That our bishops, priests, religious, and laity everywhere will give their lives for you, dear Jesus, totally, prayerfully, unreservedly, and with a spirit of sacrifice.

Vocations:

That many youth may heed your invitation: "Come, follow me."

That those already in the priestly and religious life will persevere in their vocation and will ever seek to grow in holiness.

That those who receive the sacrament of Matrimony may grow in holiness and witness to a truly Christian family life.

∞ *Pause • Reflect • Pray* ∞

Particular Intentions

I pray, dear Jesus, for:
My loved ones, parents, relatives, friends.
Those who pray for me and ask for my prayers.
The people with whom I work.
The afflicted, sorrowful, sad, lonely people in life—
whether known or unknown to me.
Those who misunderstand my motives.
Those who in all sincerity oppose me.
The souls of the faithful departed.
My loved ones in purgatory, who are often so easily
    forgotten.

∞ *Pause • Reflect • Pray* ∞

My Personal Needs

Dear Jesus, most humbly I ask for:
A deep faith, a firm hope, and an ardent love for you. I ask this through the intercession of our loving Mother Mary.

The grace to persevere until death and the grace of a blessed death in the dearest Lord. The conviction that death is a great step and the most important moment of my life—the beginning of a new life, not the ending of life.

The spirit of prayer, and the awareness of God in my life. A sense of sorrow for sin and a determination to avoid all sin so as to keep my soul ever pure in the sight of God.

The grace to have peace of soul, arising from trust in God and from living one day at a time.

The prudence to leave my life in God's hands, doing all that I can, but remembering that he is the Way and the Truth and the Life.

The grace of a devotion to the Holy Spirit, the Spirit of Truth, the Consoler and the Advocate, the Source of strength, who comes to me in Baptism—with faith, hope, and love—and in Confirmation, with his gifts of wisdom, understanding, knowledge, counsel, piety, fortitude, and fear of the Lord. The grace to love and have deep devotion to our Lady, the Mother of the Eucharistic Lord, and our spiritual Mother.

The courage to imitate her and depend upon her.

The grace to consecrate myself and my family, my work, and my problems to Mary, our Lady of the most Blessed Sacrament.

Suggested Readings from Sacred Scripture

"Whenever you pray, go into your room and shut the door and pray to your Father who is in secret; and your Father who sees in secret will reward you." (Mt 6:5–15)

" . . . If two of you agree on earth about anything you ask, it will be done for you by my Father in heaven." (Mt 18:19–20)

. . . Jesus said to him, "What do you want me to do for you?" The blind man said to him, "My teacher, let me see again." Jesus said to him, "Go; your faith has made you well." Immediately he regained his sight. . . . (Mk 10:46–52)

"I say to you, ask and it will be given you; search, and you will find; knock, and the door will be opened for you." (Lk 11:1–13)

Closing Thoughts

I will ever remember the time I have spent with you, dearest Lord, "God with us." It has been a time of grace, strength, comfort, and understanding. Before leaving let me tell you, dear Jesus, of my desire to return so that I may be strengthened in my faith, deepened in my hope, and inflamed with love for your divine presence. I will recall Benediction of the most Blessed Sacrament as I recite reverently the closing prayers.

O Salutaris

O Saving Victim opening wide,
The gate of heaven to us below;
Our foes press on from every side
Thine aid supply, thy strength bestow.

To thy great name be endless praise,
Immortal Godhead, one in three.
O grant us endless length of days,
In our true native land with thee. Amen.

Tantum Ergo

Bowing low, then offer homage
To a sacrament so great!
Here is new and perfect worship
All the old must terminate
Senses cannot grasp this marvel—
Faith must serve to compensate.

Glory, honor, adoration
Let us sing with one accord!
Praised be God, almighty Father;
Praised be Christ, His Son our Lord;
Praised be God, the Holy Spirit;
Triune Godhead be adored! Amen.

(Pause)

You have given us Bread from heaven.
Containing in itself all sweetness.

O God, who, in this wonderful sacrament has left us a memorial of your passion; grant us, we beseech you, so to venerate the sacred mysteries of your Body and Blood, that we may ever feel within us the fruit of your redemption. Who live and reign world without end. Amen.

As at Benediction, Lord, please impart your special blessings, which I will receive in prayerful humility, for myself and my loved ones.

Humbly I recite your divine praises in reparation for the neglect and irreverence shown to you in the most Blessed Sacrament:

Blessed be God.
Blessed be his Holy Name.
Blessed be Jesus Christ, true God and true Man.
Blessed be the name of Jesus.
Blessed be his most Sacred Heart.
Blessed be his most precious Blood.
Blessed be Jesus in the Most Holy Sacrament
    of the altar.
Blessed be the Holy Spirit, the Paraclete.
Blessed be the great Mother of God, Mary most holy.
Blessed be her holy and Immaculate Conception.
Blessed be her glorious Assumption.

Blessed be the name of Mary, Virgin and Mother.
Blessed be Saint Joseph, her most chaste spouse.
Blessed be God in his angels and in his saints.

∽ *Pause • Reflect • Pray* ∾

Closing Prayer to the Blessed Sacrament

As this visit of adoration closes, O Jesus, I renew my faith and trust in you. I am refreshed after these moments with you, and I count myself among a privileged number, even as your disciples were, who shared your actual presence.

Realizing that my visit to you is of little avail unless I try to live a better life and set a better example, I am resolved to go forth again to my duties and my concerns with a renewed spirit of perseverance and good will. In my daily life I will try to love and serve God well and love my neighbor also, for these two things go together. I intend to be a true disciple. Help me, O Jesus, in this resolution.

Bless me, dear Lord, before I go. And bless not only me, O Lord, but also all who are here present and all who could not come, especially the sick and the dying. Bless our homes and our children. Bless us through all our life, especially at the hour of our death.

Grant rest to the souls of the faithful departed and bring them into the light of your divine glory. So may we, who have worshiped you and been blessed by you here on earth, come to behold the radiant glory of your unveiled countenance in heaven for ever and ever. Amen.

Final Prayer

My Jesus, I must leave you now, but I will yearn to return. May I love you ever present in the Eucharist. May I always treasure the holy sacrifice of the Mass, receive you devoutly in Holy Communion, and adore you present in the most Blessed Sacrament.

My final words are addressed to your Eucharistic heart:

O divine Jesus, left alone in so many tabernacles, without visitors or worshippers, I offer you my loving heart. May every beat of my heart be a prayer of love for you. You are always watching under the sacramental veil; in your love you never sleep, and you never weary of your vigil for sinners.

O lovely Jesus! May my heart be a lamp whose light shall ever burn for you. Amen.

Eucharistic heart of Jesus, furnace of divine charity, give peace to the world.

Part II

VISITS WITH OUR LADY

Opening Thoughts

"'Here is your son. . . . Here is your mother' (Jn 19:27). These were the last words that Jesus Christ addressed to any creature before his death; they are his last will. By them he entrusted all his disciples to his own beloved Mother as her spiritual children, and he gave her to all his disciples as their spiritual Mother. Mary has by grace been exalted above all angels and men to a place second only to her Son, as the most holy Mother of God who was involved in the mysteries of Christ: she is rightly honored by a special cult in the Church" (Vatican Council II, Dogmatic Constitution on the Church).

A. To Jesus Through Mary

I Turn to Mary, My Mother

Having visited with your divine Son, O Mary, my Mother, I turn now to you with a heart filled to overflowing with thanksgiving, filial love, and tender devotion. You who are the Mother of God, please accept the humble prayers of love, reparation, and supplication that I offer to Jesus through your Immaculate Heart, that heart ever united to the Sacred Heart of my Lord and Savior, Jesus Christ.

O most beautiful Mother, Fruitful Vine, Splendor of Heaven, Singular Vessel of the Holy Spirit, hear my prayer as I kneel before you. O Mary, Empress of Heaven, from the bottom of my heart I beg of you to hear my prayers and obtain for me the graces and favors I ask during this visit. If what I ask is not for the glory of God or the salvation of my soul, I ask for peace of mind and what is most conducive to both.

To Our Lady of the Most Blessed Sacrament

As I kneel here in the presence of your Son, Jesus, my thoughts turn to you, his Mother, under the title of Lady of the Most Blessed Sacrament. I address to you my prayer of strong faith and fervent petition:

Virgin Immaculate, Mother of Jesus and my Mother, I invoke you under the title of our Lady of the Most Blessed Sacrament, because you are the Mother of the Savior who lives in the Eucharist. From you he took flesh and blood, which he feeds me in Holy Communion. I invoke you under that title also because the grace of the Eucharist comes to me through you, since you are the Mediatrix through whom God's graces reach me. And finally, I call you Our Lady of the Most Blessed Sacrament because you were the first to live the Eucharistic life. Teach me to pray the Mass as you did, to receive Holy Communion worthily and frequently, and to visit devoutly with your Son, Jesus, in the Blessed Sacrament.

∽ Pause • Reflect • Pray ∽

B. Act of Reparation to the Immaculate Heart of Mary

O most holy Virgin and our beloved Mother, I contemplate with grief the sorrow of your Immaculate Heart, surrounded with the thorns that ungrateful people place therein at every moment by their sins and ingratitude. Moved by the ardent desire of loving you as our Mother and of promoting a true devotion to your Immaculate Heart, I kneel at your feet in sorrow for the grief that people cause you. I want to atone by my prayers and sacrifices for the offenses you so often receive, despite your tender love for us.

Obtain for me and for everyone the pardon of our sins. A word from you will obtain grace and forgiveness for us all. Hasten, O Lady, the conversion of sinners that they may love Jesus and cease to offend God while on earth, and thus enjoy him forever in heaven. Amen.

C. Rosary of the Blessed Virgin

"The Church has always attributed particular efficacy to this prayer, entrusting to the Rosary, to its choral recitation and to its constant practice, the most difficult problems. At times when Christianity itself seemed under threat, its deliverance was attributed to the power of this prayer, and Our Lady of the Rosary was acclaimed as the one whose intercession brought salvation. Today I willingly entrust to the power of this prayer . . . the cause of peace in the world and the cause of the family" (Pope John Paul II, On the Most Holy Rosary).

Offering of My Intentions

Eternal Father, I offer you this rosary, through the most pure heart of Mary in union with the precious Blood of Jesus Christ, in thanksgiving for all your benefits, in atonement for my sins, for the needs of your holy Church, the desires of the Sacred Heart of Jesus, and for all those graces and blessings that will keep me close to that loving heart in life, in death, in time, and for eternity, and especially for. . .

THE JOYFUL MYSTERIES

    1. The Annunciation

    2. The Visitation

    3. The Nativity

    4. The Presentation

    5. The Finding of Jesus in the Temple

THE LUMINOUS MYSTERIES
1. The Baptism of Jesus
2. Jesus Reveals His Glory at the Wedding of Cana
3. Jesus Preaches the Kingdom and Calls Us to Conversion
4. The Transfiguration
5. Jesus Gives us the Eucharist

THE SORROWFUL MYSTERIES
1. The Agony in the Garden
2. The Scourging at the Pillar
3. The Crowning with Thorns
4. The Carrying of the Cross
5. The Crucifixion

THE GLORIOUS MYSTERIES
1. The Resurrection
2. The Ascension
3. The Descent of the Holy Spirit
4. The Assumption of Our Lady into Heaven
5. The Coronation of Our Lady

Queen of the most holy Rosary, pray for us.

Closing Thoughts

O Mary, my Mother, I must leave now, but I implore you to stay with me as you are ever with your divine Son,

Jesus. He has given you all power over his heart. Take me, your child, and place me in his divine heart, so that my soul may be purified from all that is displeasing to him, so that from now on my heart may be like yours in the love of God and of my neighbor.

O Mary, Mother of my Savior, I love you!

O Mary, delight of the Holy Spirit, I hope in your maternal intercession!

O Mary, chosen by God the Father, you are queen of my heart!

O Lady, Queen of heaven, my Mother Mary, by your love for Jesus and for me, I beg you to obtain for me one more grace: never to let pass an opportunity of serving you, and to persevere in fervor until death. Amen.

Part III

PRAYERS AND READINGS

A. Prayers of Devotion

I. To Our Lady of
the Most Blessed Sacrament

Virgin Mary, Our Lady of the Most Blessed
    Sacrament,
glory of the Christian people,
joy of the universal Church,
hope of the world, pray for us.

And ask the Holy Spirit to enkindle in the hearts of
    the faithful
devotion to the most Holy Eucharist,
that they may be worthy
to receive Jesus daily.
Our Lady of the Most Blessed Sacrament,
    pray for us.

2. The Magnificat

My soul magnifies the Lord, and my spirit rejoices in
God, my Savior.

For he has regarded the humility of his handmaid; for
behold, from henceforth all generations will call
me blessed:

For he who is mighty has done great things for me;
and holy is his name;

And his mercy is from generation to generation on
those who fear him.

He has shown might in his arm; he has scattered the
proud in the conceit of their hearts.

He has put down the mighty from their seats and has
exalted the humble.

He has filled the hungry with good things and the
rich he has sent away empty.

He has received Israel, his servant; being mindful of
his mercy;

As he spoke to our fathers, to Abraham, and to his
children forever.

3. To Our Lady Queen of Angels

August Queen of heaven! Sovereign mistress of the
angels! You who from the beginning have received from

God the power and mission to crush the head of Satan; we humbly beseech you to send your holy legions that under your command and by your power, they may pursue the evil spirits, encounter them on every side, resist their bold attacks and drive them far away from us into the abyss of everlasting woe. Amen.

4. The Memorare

Remember, O most gracious Virgin Mary, that never was it known that anyone who fled to your protection, implored your help, or sought your intercession was left unaided. Inspired with this confidence, I fly to you, O Virgin of virgins, my Mother; to you I come; before you I stand, sinful and sorrowful. O Mother of the Word Incarnate, despise not my petitions, but in your mercy hear and answer me. Amen.

5. To Saint Joseph

O guardian and father of virgins, to whose faithful custody were entrusted innocence itself, Jesus Christ and Mary the Virgin of virgins, I pray and beseech you through Jesus and Mary, that being preserved from uncleanness, I may with spotless mind, pure heart, and chaste body serve them most chastely all the days of my life. Amen.

6. To My Guardian Angel

Angel of God, my guardian dear,
To whom God's love commits me here,
Ever this day be at my side
To light and guard, to rule and guide. Amen.

7. Morning Prayer

O Divine Master, you are my shield and protection. You are my Good Shepherd, my guide and my strength. I stand before you in need of your protection. Teach me to hold myself in silence before you and adore you in the depths of my soul. Help me to listen to you always and never do anything displeasing to you. I do not know what will happen to me today, but I do know nothing can happen to me without your knowledge. I accept all that in union with you, my Lord. I beg of you only one thing: the grace to wait upon you always and never ask anything of you but the fulfillment of your will. Teach me to let you act in me. May I do nothing for my self-esteem or praise, but only for the glory of you, my Master. Amen.

B. Prayers for Special Intentions

1. For the Faithful Departed

Remember, O Lord, all the faithful who have departed this life. Grant them rest in the bosom of our fathers Abraham, Isaac, and Jacob; feed them in green pastures, by the waters of comfort in the paradise of joy. Give them release from broken hearts, sorrows, and sighs. We ask this through Jesus Christ our Lord. Amen.

2. For the Gifts of the Holy Spirit

O plenteous source of every good and perfect gift, enrich our hearts with the consoling light of your seven-fold grace. Fill us with the gifts of wisdom, understanding, counsel, fortitude, knowledge, piety, and holy fear of the Lord. Yes, Spirit of love and gentleness, most humbly do we implore your assistance! You know our faults, our understanding, the waywardness of our affections, and the weakness of our will. Therefore, when we neglect to practice what we know, visit us, we beseech you, with your grace. Enlighten our minds, O God; purify our desires; correct our wanderings and pardon our omissions, so that by your guidance, we may live in good conscience and eventually reach the heaven of eternal peace. This we ask through Jesus Christ our Lord. Amen.

3. For Our Holy Father

O God, Shepherd and Ruler of all the faithful, look with favor upon your servant Pope . . . , whom you have appointed pastor of your Church. Grant that by word and example he may assist those whom he serves, so that the shepherd and the flock entrusted to his care may together attain everlasting life. We ask this through Jesus Christ our Lord. Amen.

4. For Peace

O God, who authors all holy desires, right counsels, and just works, give to your servants that peace which the world cannot give; dispose our hearts to obey your commandments and shelter us so that, once the fear of enemies has been removed, our times may be peaceful. We ask this through our Lord Jesus Christ, your Son, who lives and reigns with you in the unity of the Holy Spirit, God, world without end. Amen.

5. A Prayer for Priests
By Richard Cardinal Cushing

Almighty God, look upon the face of him who is the eternal High Priest, and have compassion on your priests in today's world. Remember that they are weak and frail human beings. Stir up in them the grace of their vocation.

Keep them close to you lest the enemy prevail against them, so that they may never do anything in the slightest degree unworthy of their sublime vocation.

O Jesus, I pray for your faithful and fervent priests, for the unfaithful and tepid ones, for those laboring at home and abroad in distant mission fields, for those who are tempted, for those who are lonely and desolate, for those who are young, for those who are dying, and for those who are in purgatory.

But, above all, I recommend to you the priests dearest to me: the priest who baptized me, the priests who absolved me from my sins, the priests at whose Masses I have assisted and who gave me your Body and Blood in Holy Communion, the priests who instructed me or helped me by their encouragement. I pray for all the priests to whom I am indebted in any other way, in particular for. . . . O Jesus, keep them all close to your heart and bless them abundantly in time and in eternity. Amen.

O Mary, Queen of the clergy, pray for us; obtain for us many and holy priests.

6. For Special Blessings

Bless my memory, that it may ever recollect you.

Bless my understanding, that it may ever think of you.

Bless my will, that it may never seek or desire that which displeases you.

Bless my body and all its actions.

Bless my heart with all its affections.

Bless me now and at the hour of my death.

Dear Savior, in the days of your mortal life, you showed your love and preference for the poor and the lowly, the suffering and the sick. Give solace to those who are in poverty and want; console and strengthen the sick and bring consolation to those who mourn the loss of dear ones.

Bless in particular, dear Jesus, those who have strayed from the true fold and lead them back to the haven of peace.

Bless and comfort missionaries, who are far from home and their loved ones.

Bless the priests laboring in this portion of the vineyard.

Bless us all and grant that as now we are gathered about your altar, we may one day be gathered about your throne in heaven.

7. To Saint Joseph for Strength

To you, O blessed Joseph, do we hasten in our trouble; and having implored the help of your holy spouse, we confidently invoke your patronage also. By that affection that united you to the Immaculate Virgin, Mother of God, and by that fatherly love with which you embraced the Child Jesus, we humbly beseech you to look with favor upon the heritage that Jesus Christ has won for us by his blood. By your power and aid strengthen us in our need.

O most wise guardian of the Holy Family, protect the chosen people of Jesus Christ. O most loving father, keep us from all blight of sin and corruption. O most mighty deliverer, from your place in heaven mercifully help us in this struggle with the powers of darkness. And even as of old you saved the Child Jesus from the danger of death, so now defend God's holy Church from the wiles of the enemy and from all adversity.

Keep each and all of us under your perpetual patronage so that, sustained by your example and your help, we may be able to live in holiness, die in sanctity, and attain everlasting happiness in heaven.

C. Prayerful Aspirations

May the Sacred Heart of Jesus be loved in every place.
Sweet Heart of Jesus, grant that I may ever love you
    more.
Heart of Jesus, burning with love for us, inflame
    our hearts with love for you.
Heart of Jesus, I put my trust in you.
Jesus, meek and humble of heart, make my heart
    like unto yours.
All for you, most sweet heart of Jesus.

Sacred Heart of Jesus, I believe in your love for me.

Sacred Heart of Jesus, protect our families.

O Mary, conceived without sin, pray for us who
have recourse to you.

Immaculate Heart of Mary, pray for us.

Our Lady of Fatima, pray for us.

Our Lady of the Most Blessed Sacrament,
pray for us.

O Sacrament most holy, O Sacrament divine.

All praise and all thanksgiving, be every moment
thine.

Sacred Heart of Jesus, be my salvation;
sweet Heart of Mary, be my love.

D. Additional Readings from Sacred Scripture

Adoration

FROM THE GOSPEL ACCORDING TO SAINT MATTHEW

We have seen his star (2:1–12)

The Baptism of Jesus (3:16–17)

The temptation in the desert (4:1–11)

Jesus walks on the lake (14:22–33)

Peter's confession of faith (16:13–20)

The Transfiguration (17:1–8)

Sorrow

Forgiving others (18:21–35)
Peter's denial (26:69–75)

FROM THE GOSPEL ACCORDING TO SAINT MARK

Jesus cures the paralytic and forgives
    sins (2:3–12)

FROM THE GOSPEL ACCORDING TO SAINT LUKE

John the Baptist cries: repent! (3:1–18)
Jesus eats with sinners (5:27–32)
Love your enemies (6:27–45)
The woman who was a sinner (7:36–50)
Examples inviting repentance (13:1–5)
The prodigal son (15:11–32)
The Pharisee and the publican (18:9–14)
The good thief (23:39–43)

FROM THE GOSPEL ACCORDING TO SAINT JOHN

The adulteress (8:1–11)
Slaves of sin (8:31–36)

Thanksgiving

FROM THE GOSPEL ACCORDING TO SAINT MATTHEW

Jesus rejoices (11:25–27)
Jesus fulfills the prophecies (12:16–21)
Miracle of the loaves and fishes (14:15–21)

FROM THE GOSPEL ACCORDING TO SAINT MARK

The true brothers and sisters of Jesus (3:31–35)
The apostles leave all for Christ (10:28–31)
The Eucharist (14:22–25)

FROM THE GOSPEL ACCORDING TO LUKE

Visitation and our Lady's Magnificat (1:39–79)
Simeon (2:25–32)
In the synagogue in Nazareth (4:16–22)
The disciples return rejoicing (10:17–24)
The ten lepers cured (17:11–19)

FROM THE GOSPEL ACCORDING TO SAINT JOHN

Jesus' gift of the Eucharist and eternal life (6:32–40)

Petition

FROM THE GOSPEL ACCORDING TO MATTHEW

Pray in secret; the Our Father (6:5–15)
Leper and centurion (8:1–13)
The two blind men (9:27–31)
Have faith like a mustard seed (17:14–20)
If two or three ask anything (18:19–20)

FROM THE GOSPEL ACCORDING TO SAINT MARK

Daughter of Jairus; woman with a hemorrhage
(5:21–43)
Faith of the Canaanite woman (7:24–30)

Cure of the boy (9:14–29)
Blind man at Jericho (10:46–52)
Parable of fig tree (11:20–25)

FROM THE GOSPEL ACCORDING TO LUKE

The centurion's servant (7:1–10)
Our Father, ask, knock, seek (11:1–13)
The judge and the importunate widow (18:1–8)

FROM THE GOSPEL ACCORDING TO SAINT JOHN

Ask in the name of Jesus (14:12–14)
Abide in God; then ask what you will (15:7–16)
Ask in the name of Jesus (16:20–24)

BOOKS & MEDIA

The Daughters of St. Paul operate book and media centers at the following addresses. Visit, call, or write the one nearest you today, or find us at www.pauline.org

California
3908 Sepulveda Blvd, Culver City, CA 90230 — 310-397-8676
935 Brewster Avenue, Redwood City, CA 94063 — 650-369-4230
5945 Balboa Avenue, San Diego, CA 92111 — 858-565-9181

Florida
145 S.W. 107th Avenue, Miami, FL 33174 — 305-559-6715

Hawaii
1143 Bishop Street, Honolulu, HI 96813 — 808-521-2731

Illinois
172 North Michigan Avenue, Chicago, IL 60601 — 312-346-4228

Louisiana
4403 Veterans Memorial Blvd, Metairie, LA 70006 — 504-887-7631

Massachusetts
885 Providence Hwy, Dedham, MA 02026 — 781-326-5385

Missouri
9804 Watson Road, St. Louis, MO 63126 — 314-965-3512

New York
64 W. 38th Street, New York, NY 10018 — 212-754-1110

South Carolina
243 King Street, Charleston, SC 29401 — 843-577-0175

Virginia
1025 King Street, Alexandria, VA 22314 — 703-549-3806

Canada
3022 Dufferin Street, Toronto, ON M6B 3T5 — 416-781-9131